When I read Mar Ka's poems, I'm reminded of the way I've often felt while standing on a ridge looking down at a single animal track crossing a snow-covered marsh. A blue light flickers in the track making it appear to be a burning wick. Night is coming on. For a moment, I'm transformed, lifted out of myself. Good poetry can do that…One of my favorites in this collection tells us that the Ancient Greeks believed that humans throw light. Mar Ka's poems throw light even when the subject is dark, when "Something has rotted, wormed by greed." She sees the world with a clear eye. If you're going to read only one book by an Alaskan poet this year, read this book. Mar Ka knows Alaska and its Native people like few poets I've read. If you're looking for a sense of Alaska as a place conveyed through vivid imagery, you'll find it here. If you're looking for a deeply human and appealing voice, you'll find it here. This is a collection to be read. It's a powerful book.

—Tom Sexton, former Alaska Poet Laureate, is the author of ten books of poetry including *Li Bai Rides a Celestial Dolphin Home.*

Be-hooved by Alaskan poet Mar Ka journeys through the north with a sharp eye and ear and brilliant verbal gifts. These poems carry the reader forward like the migrating caribou that populate its pages. Exploring and recording this lovely but threatened landscape, it's a book to treasure and re-read.

—John Morgan, author of seven books of poetry including *Archives of the Air* and *River of Light: A Conversation with Kabir.*

In her luminous debut collection, Mar Ka navigates the north through incantatory poems of responsibility and connection—to land, to animal, to story, self, and one another. Chasing the lights through long Alaskan nights, these poems drum like caribou hooves, carrying "the thrum of hearts through bone and bark and stone." With a revelatory power of witness, discerning nature's elemental songs, she asks us what it means to be wild, convincing us that to be more human, we also need to be more hooved. *Be-Hooved* maps the foreign and familiar corners of home.

—Chip Livingston, author of *Crow-Blue, Crow-Black* and *Owls Don't Have to Mean Death.*

Well crafted turns and wonderful surprises . . . especially the surprises, which for me are always at the heart of good poetry.

—J. Edward Chamberlin, author of twelve books, including *A Covenant in Wonder with the World: The Power of Stories and Songs* and *The Banker and the Blackfoot: An Untold Story of Friendship, Trust, and Broken Promises in the Old West.*

Mar Ka's collection *Be-hooved* evokes an Alaskan wilderness that I haven't seen in poems before, addressing directly the effects of global warming without ever falling into lecture. There is warning here but also joy, attachment, wonder. Mar Ka is skilled with subtle rhyme and her line is compelling—one poem pulls me into the next and the next, and I find new images to admire in each reading. *Be-hooved* is news from the climate change front, an accessible collection that deserves a wide audience.

—Kathleen Flenniken, former Washington State Poet Laureate, author of the poetry collections *Famous* and *Plume.*

I have read this collection three times . . . I find the music of the line in each poem compelling. Strong images: caribou, cold, glaciers, migration, death of species . . . Poems speak back and forth to each other, addressing the consequences of environmental issues; survival of the species and people; defining a place called 'home'; faith and spirituality in a landscape that can be unforgiving, and the significance of memory and story-telling. I was struck by the poems that challenge ownership of place. Who is responsible for nature's survival? Who is responsible for human survival? What happens when the balance of nature is altered? Are there really accidents?

—M.J. Iuppa, author of four poetry collections, most recently *This Thirst.*

BE-
HOOVED

poems by Mar Ka

All the proceeds from this book are being donated to indigenous and environmental organizations.

Text © 2019 University of Alaska Press

Published by
University of Alaska Press
P.O. Box 756240
Fairbanks, AK 99775-6240

Cover design by UA Press.

Cover art by Sonya Kelliher-Combs, *Remnant (Caribou Antler)*, 2016. Mixed media, organic and synthetic materials. Photograph by Chris Arend.

Interior design by Jen Gunderson, 590 Design.
Interior photographs by Mary Kancewick.

Library of Congress Cataloging in Publication Data

Names: Mar-Ka, author.
Title: Be-hooved / by Mar-Ka.
Description: Fairbanks, AK: University of Alaska Press, 2019. |
Identifiers: LCCN 2018028793 (print) | LCCN 2018029128 (ebook) | ISBN
   9781602233775 (ebook) | ISBN 9781602233768 (pbk.: alk. paper)
Classification: LCC PS3613.A69 (ebook) | LCC PS3613.A69 A6 2019 (print) | DDC
   811/.6dc23
LC record available at https://lccn.loc.gov/2018028793

*In gratitude to the lands and peoples
of Alaska for shaping the consciousness
expressed in these poems.*

We'd rather have the iceberg than the ship,

although it meant the end of travel.

…

Icebergs behoove the soul.

—Elizabeth Bishop

For surefooted step, hooves behoove the haver.

—Hannah Sanghee Park

To learn you must be open, diligent, and willing to be an individual.

…

Examine the distortion and effects of the warming earth.

—Dg Nanouk Okpik

CONTEXT IS EVERYTHING

I

II

III

IV

AN AFTERWORD

ROADS

End of the road.
Just a thought,
until I came here.

Here, all of them—
roads—have ends you
come to. I came to

understand that
to go on,
I need to change

modes. It's a step
into self,
where roads continue

as long as you
follow them: Roads, here,
are yes-long . . .

Caribou have been on the North American continent for as long as two million years . . . have survived multiple ice ages . . . while other mammals became extinct.

—Monte Hummel and Justina C. Ray, *Caribou and the North: A Shared Future*

COLD AND CARIBOU ARE LOVERS

Those adaptations that meld lovers, those micro-adjustments / to each other, let us call them language, call them / poems, call them songs. Listen to the singing fur of the caribou— / the felted underfur, the whistling guard-hair tubes of Arctic breath— / hear them chime against cold wind, buoy against cold water, rest / against frozen ground. Contemplate, now, the throb of how / caribou swell onto the lap of the wind-whipped Arctic / plain, coated in that singing, the sweet-fuzzed muzzle notes building / to pert, fluffed codas, trilling down stick legs where the tremolos / of arteries and veins track side-by-side, like ensemble sections, / heart-fired arterial ichor beating, heating returning venous blood / in torso-to-toe cold harmonization. Hear how, winters, / hair between shrunken toes grows in volume, in seasonal vibrato, / as at the subtle gestures of a maestro's baton, a soft / pinging within the singing bowls of horn hooves used / in creatively improvised percussion, cymbals, banging / light and wide on snow, on mud over permafrost; seasonally / hollowed, sharply edged, for striking ice like a triangle shattered / over crisped lichens, lipped into whisks. Listen, now, to the thrown / kisses of ankle tendons clicking over bone, kiss-kiss, kiss-kiss, / the castanets keeping herds close in all conditions. Listen / to gelid air drawn through coiled nose-horns, warmed—and read: / the planetary notes of chemicals, the molecular trills, / the signatures linking calves to cows, the musical phrases / of compounds unspooling unknowns, giving time / signature to food, to predators—wolf, bear, human. Fall / deep into the tones of caribou eyes, echo chambers singing ultraviolet, / soloing forage, predator urine streams, slinking, stalking predator / forms; sink into eyes that during the long dark become / a thousand times more sensitive to light, to shadings. / The cold and the caribou, they lean into each other's arms. /

A SHADOW

is made up of old
heady days

of trying to hold
the time

the antlered blossom

when it reaches
the ground

IMPLICATED

(i)

Hundreds of thousands
of white-bellied common murre corpses
pile on beaches. And inland, too,
far from evolved-for habitats.
No fat under skins, nothing
in gastrointestinal tracts. Breeding
colonies deserted. Wastelands.
It's happening, it's happening . . .
Warming waters, implicated
in food resource changes, proliferation
of toxic algae blooms.

(ii)

Between boardwalks, houses
built on permafrost sink into puddles.
Storms swallow the low-lying, pond-pocked land
looped by river and slough.
All its crying Jonahs: Look here!
Boats bob in rising floodwaters, the Noahs
floating-floating-floating. Dashed.
Disbelieving and undelivered.
Freshwater sources disappearing,
compromised by salt. Hold that irony:
Finger that stone worry.

(iii)

Thawing permafrost mires
caribou; warming temperatures favor
insect-parasites; a lengthened wildfire season
burns forage to ashes;
freezing rains, in autumn, lock lichens
under super-thick ice; coastal plain green-up,
the most nutrition-rich stage,
occurs now before cows arrive.
Note, too, the First Peoples'
intimate reliance, what it bodes
for what grows thin.

I

POST-CALVING
COLD SEEKING

From Arctic coastal tundra calving plains, / caribou aggregates seek ridgetop chill winds, / seek remnant patches of cooling snow and ice, / seek relief from herd-sized clouds of biting insects, / from the mosquitoes that suck and welt, / from the flies that burrow in, maggot out. / As calves strengthen, aggregates disperse / become mobile bands that seek cold niches as ardently / as they seek the calories of ground lichens. / It is the caress of coolness that calms herd movements; / it is the cold slap that has their 'bou-backs. /

UTQIAĠVIK BEACH WALK

—for Eileen Panigeo MacLean

Nine-month shore ice floats broken
on the horizon of the sea
nobody owns. I walk

in the sun all night, in the wind
that pushed or carried the ice,
on the black sand beach, following

the ruts of three-wheelers,
looking for old things still of enough
shape to recognize, among

things all old and broken
and polished into fineness
and such seeming sameness I

must kneel and palm and finger
to isolate the different
glitters, the shifts in colors,

the quality of grit, the sighing
solubility of particle,
the ability to ride

the wave, the wind. All night
my eyes, my skin, test what is.
In this place where summer

is no dark, day no end, and hidden
in the people's bones are diaries
of thousands of years of drumming songs,

there is this light wing of my life
dusting things, caressing
and tickling, there is this sensation—

of something happening.

RAVEN

The flint-eyed raven probes each knuckled ridge
along the earth's knotted spine,

follows wolves following caribou, knows
the color red, the honey of blood, drops

wings slowly, like snow, clutches
gift-flesh, makes sounds that tear, sounds that

knock ribs like elbows. I imagine
    a painting:
Still Life with Raven in Window.

WHAT IS WILD?

—After this poem was written,
the Migratory Bird Treaty Act was amended
to allow a spring hunt of migratory birds
for Alaska Natives.

In Anchorage, at Josephine's haute cuisine restaurant,

we two women note swan drawings, on door, on menu.

Trumpeters have long teemed here, banking west and north

each spring—from the country of Napoléon, his Empress—

to nest, collect eyrars, return refreshed to lakes of palaces.

Then, I reflect, Yupik women used thin lengths of black

from swan-leg skin to sinew-sew line designs

into clothing seams. Slender strips of water-tested leather;

dark streams smooth-edging caribou-hide continents.

Today, as advised by the queen previous to Empress Josephine,

we rabble prepare to eat cake, drink coffee. The curved-necked

silver pot on our table empties. We pay homage to the *qugyuk*

by sounding the lamentations in our chests. She says she tells

the ugly duckling tale to girls who doubt their swan-selves.

I say I watched a woman in Alakanuk pluck a swan

on a kitchen floor, saving the down for a daughter's pillow,

the wings for feather-dusting; boiling the meat, with greens,

for sweet-eating. All banned now, by migratory bird treaties.

My friend talks of holding tightly to shaking children, listening
to mothers cry. Scars, like stars, seem, to those who view
from afar, she says, cold, though pain blazes with white heat.
I speak of testimony, transcripts, laws. Of explaining; trying
to understand. I think: Tired neck, heavy breast, aching wings.

I open the menu the server has left. See, among the starters,
broiled loin of lion. When he next comes near, I ask,
More coffee, more cream, and, sir, lion from where?
Coffee poured, cream proffered, he answers, *We serve surplus*
zoo animals here. More dessert, ladies? I ponder—zoo swans?

To my friend I proffer a stone flower from the shores
of the Chukchi Sea, say that the movement of flowers blooming
is a kind of slow flying; that even stone petals, at their glacial
pace, echo swans, and dying. I think—What is wild?

We gather up our things. Over the still snow-covered hillside,
a pulse of wings. Strokes in counterpoint flight. Plumage
of that so-rare-in-nature unblemished white. Slender necks held
straight out. I say how I love that a female swan—for her large,
stiff, wing-feathers, which make such fine quills—is called a pen.

VILLAGE ASCENSION

— in response to "Bypassing Rue Descartes" by Czesław Miłosz,
for Thomas Berger and Dalee Sambo

I ascend from the river, shy, an intruder,
a non-native person just come to a Native village.

Ashamed to remember the habits of my house
I accept a stew of leftover fall caribou from strangers, wipe my plate clean.
Keep quiet. Keep counsel. Keep trying

to understand what is being misunderstood.
I enter the woods blinded by shade, disoriented.

What options, ways, present themselves? Cut down
the tree? Climb one into sun? Wait for eyes
to adjust to given light?

Meanwhile the village behaves in accordance with its summer nature,
sleeping and waking all hours in the all-hour light,
checking salmon nets in bear-gun weighted boats,
cleaning, cutting, drying the fish gathered like manna—

indifferent to progress, productivity, rising GNPs,
all tended by others in other countries
with different religions and different heavens,
different songs, dances, and things called serpents.

WOMEN BOATING

—Point Hope, Alaska, 1980s

an open skin boat
geese overhead
a seal
leading

we move our limbs
in rays, our paddles
in ripples
our faces

in season
our voices
in the time
that moves all

together   we are
the *nanogak*—
women
boating

bract-held   relicts
blooming the moment
towing ghosts
and gods

TRANSFORMATION

I brought north two cats, urban house pets.
One jumped a sled dog, which broke its neck,
lies now in a bed of last year's leaves
in the deep hollow of a very old, very
rotted spruce tree. I sealed the den
with muddy sand, on break-up day,
break-up day in the evening.

The cat that lives is sand-bellied gravel,
alder limbs, the shadow under winter grass,
spruce trunk flecked with sun.
The cat that lives is the red squirrel
eaten head first, guts, feet, tail—
all up to the last mited bite of fur;
is the spruce grouse, heart first,
breast-down lifted into wind on whiskers;
is the sparrow swallowed whole, nearly.

That transformation, the dance
of chance and grace, delicate balance—
sandpipers loving slough bank,
song-shaping throats of thrush,
the fine forever spin of water
being sucked into a round melting.
The trick: casting the glance, the claw,

flicking the head, snagging the eyes,
hooking the mouth, nose, ears, arms held wide,
faster, lightly, flinging widely
sense after sense after sense, drawing
in the joy, holding always
the joy, mouthing always the joy, feeling
the suspense, the sustenance.

Thus let us winnow—like snipes,
knowing angels taught them this:
to transform wind into song
with all parts of the body, to transform
body into song, with all parts of mind,
to transform mind into song
with all parts of the wind. Watch
the iris of the cat's eye hug light: the high
note of a hymn, held. Believe
in life transformed; that we transform life
in belief; that belief transforms us.
That life is thus, to be transformed.

Let us be the sand that sings when stepped on,
that sings suspended in water,
against the side of a boat,
that sings flung by the wind
against glass, which is sand, transformed.

FIRE SEASON

—the Interior

a bit of a heat uptick
a humidity dip

lightning   strong winds
matchstick trees ignite

it's in-hand to out-of-hand
in one quick flick

a conflagration of relation
smoke signals fly

POLE POEM

—upon visiting Totem Park
in Ketchikan

I.

thunder:

the beating of

the bird's wings

lightning:

the blink

of the bird's eyes

mountains

and clouds:

the habitat

of eagles

of heroes

spirit aids

powers

II.

Raven:

recognized

by his straight

black beak carved

box of light

at his feet

Fog Woman:

labret in her lip

in her hands

the first

salmon

of time

III.

Natsihline:

by carving

brought to life

the blackfish

killer whale

carved

on his fingernails

lessons learned

sorrows   and

raptures

CREEKSIDE

Cardigan weather. The creek is my good company,
rushing below our cliff-side house with a galvanizing
energy. Wind makes river of hair, rock of head,
educing call and response from our eternally evolving
kindredness. Chaos, contained by our keening chorus.

IN-KIND

—Upper Yukon River

I sought a volunteer to motor me downstream
to the next Gwich'in village, for gas money,
making the involved time and effort
an in-kind contribution to Native advocacy outreach.
I got an angry caribou-hide-vested draftee, who,
shaking his heavy hair back, banged and muttered,
not meeting my eyes, spitting muddy chew juice
into the headwind, so that it flew at my cheek.

A rev of engine noise, and wind-whipping.

As we thrummed into flow, agitations
of water, air, spirit, rippled out in our wake.
The long jostling had its numbing, lulling, effect.
And the sun did its regenerative part.

ADDRESSING THE GLACIER

The highest part is called the head.
The most forward end is the tongue.
The front forms a high wall,
which is called the face.

Like new caribou calves, we
work at placing ourselves
on the cool lap of the glacier,
learning to use our hooves,
chasing after our mothers,
trusting in the fortitude
of immensity and age. I
feel at home
dusted with rock flour.

Nearly 100,000 glaciers
have been identified,
yet most of them
don't have names.

We name the things we own; think we
own the things we name.
Our names own us,
hold us to the world's face
as surely as crampons
grip ice and snow, as surely
as a glacier hour
holds the Holocene.

VISION DREAM

Refusing to die peacefully, becomingly,
she bursts from her house.
Heavily, screaming, she runs,
skirt wadded at her waist,
flanks gleaming in morning sun.
Sweat collects, running with her.

She returns in a caribou skin,
head capped with head,
antlers weighting her neck.
Sweat and blood streak her face.
She knocks at her door.

The body politic helps her hop:
impales her on a pole
in through woman-hole,
out through woman mouth.
Whitely naked men shoulder the skewer,
hop on one foot and then the other,
tight-spiral up the mountain. Singing.

Processions of blaze move over her animal body,
its children, they skip down each limb.
Arms and legs spread-eagled,
she reaches into space. As the pole spins,
her light illuminates everything.

THE MAN WHO MADE THINGS FROM NOTHING

—Fairbanks

The old man, her great-uncle, asked my friend, what
would you like me to make for you, little ptarmigan?
A dogsled, please, she said. He nodded. She smiled.
He went outside, found some downed trees and
with a plane he made from a stone, he shaped them.
He worked outdoors, tapped no electric flow. Showed
me how he made his drill, a stick with a nail wedged
at the end of it and a little bow, and he put the stick
in his mouth and he moved the bow, and it drilled
hole after perfect hole. He used strips from a hide he
had tanned, a hide from a moose he had killed for
its meat. And he soaked and he bent and he looped
and he stretched. And for a brake he wedged an antler.
And when the dogs, the eager dogs, pulled it, that sled,
it slid and held, bounced and swung and—lived.

UNDER A CLOUD

rain comes to the dust
        long wet fingers reaching out—
                what to make of this?

she watches the rain
        the girl   in the woman
                raising her arms

showing wet and sexy
        without within her slicked skin
                stay in stay in stay

the real people know
        from upriver   downriver
                lures and hooks and nets

gifts and gratitude
        will find her in the water
                their touch iambic

her dreaming eyes shut
        ride away girl ride away
                on the hooves of the rain

the girl in the tent
        the boreal downpour how
                it-she-they-we sing

how we sing   wet-rubbed

     like the thin rims of bowls   made

       of ore   forged

how we sing ourselves

     real   between earth and water

       dreaming   an opening

BERRY PICKING IN THE RAIN

Despite the pelting from above, the insistent bursting
upon thin-skinned impact, the tattooing with ink invisible,
yet indelible as the seeds cached within all juicy flesh,

we reach into dry darkness. Lift leafy masses with grand
sweepings. Reveal laden linings. Stain-probing fingers
persist in plucking—blue, black, red, yellow, orange.

Pails flush with fruit rest in redolent mist. We watch each
fingernail leaf—drip. Languorously. Luminously.

A damped sun sinks into the vale, calling home the berried,
emblazoning yet, the river braiding its breadth.
As with lightning, the forks and branchings are the same

in the binding power given: By breakage we are bound.
Everything lies between you and me. We reach for it
all, hold it—all—wet and bruised and sticky and sweet

in our mouths. Skies arc stardust to stardust.
We act, react, abreact, impact, tesseract . . .

In this tryst conjoined, we daughters and sons of explosion
engage, in the drench of dusk, raise our clinking buckets.
The universe holds the pail-keen that rings and rings.

ABOUT SKIES

*—for my children, inspired by a Yupik
story about a shaman's vision*

It begins this way
as you drew it

the ceilings, the skies
far away, very high.

Can you imagine that someday
your sky will press down on you?

You will crouch, squat, or kneel
but it won't stop.

You will control your panic,
move along it running your hands

firm against it, fingers measuring
the size of star holes.

You will find yours, will pull
yourself through

meet the next, and another
wonder about forever

until the final sky, crayon-colored
with stick-on stars—

Someone there will offer you
food. You will bring it

to your lips; it will kiss you
with a wet face, small palms

and wriggles. Startled, you will let
go, and be thrown through the skies

pulling past you, to wake at home,
maybe on a hill, maybe at daybreak;

maybe to make here the remembered
final pretend sky

drawing it down over children
like quilted covers,

helping small bodies to find their
star holes, standing

on tiptoe, if their arms
are strong, and reaching.

CITIZENS OF THE USA

Braids, traditional to both our cultures,
swing to the same point on our backs.
Our skin tones are a precise match: It seems
the daughter of peasant farmers can tan
as deeply as the daughter of hunter-gatherers.

She asks what tribe I am. I answer—Lithuanian.
She asks is that Athabascan. I say, no, it is
Indo-European. A raven lands nearby, making
the knocking sounds of the dominant female. We
give her space as we sink to the river's bank.

She asks whether I speak my Native language.
I say that my grandmother taught me a little.
She says, "Me, too." We know that our children
won't speak it, which is a shame and a distance.
We sound some words, to share the rhythms.

We talk of occupiers' aggressions, oppressions
of language, of culture, of religion, of thought—
the attempts to transform another into oneself
when it—when we—cannot just be bzzzt out
of being using some version of a bug zapper . . .

Flexing jointly in the sparse, weedy grass, we chat
as we work to mend the old seine net spread
over our cross-legged laps, weaving a tensile web
of words, of wonders, with knots quick, tight, even.

RIVER STONE

The stone I hold
fills my hand.

I want to tell it,
compel it,

to tell me
how to be
still within.

I feel cool rays spill
into my palm:

Not *will*, but
willing.

FOLLOWING
SNOW AND COLD

As temperatures cool, / caribou bands edge south / into the cooling, moving / with the spreading cooling / toward the tree line, toward / the snowy northern forests, / toward the wintering wood, / toward the just-right cold-dark. /

IMMORTAL LONGING

The gray blanket clouds
are equalizers, they
distribute the sun's light
evenly, so that each
turning leaf glows, holding
its measure,
returning brightness skyward.

The blazing leaves
die of immortality.

Quick comes the long dark,
long coolness, longing,
the immortal longing
to be lit from within.
We must, we must believe
it will happen again.

CARIBOU

—a response to the poem "Cow," by Federico
Garcia Lorca, for Paula Álvarez López

Pronged antlers hold the submerged rock,
or the other way around. Clouds and trees
ripple over tines.

The missing muzzle, did it flutter
under a slow moustache of slobber?
Did a red moan bring its day to its knees?

A final bellow *with half-closed eyes*, lights
like those, now, winking across the waves,
sparking the lowering curtain?

Oh fish, oh birds, oh man honing your knife
till it slides between cells, like heat, cold, rot—
did you dine on this life?

What is cloven and chews cud is clean, so
one sacred book says. Tell that to the river
that washes everything.

AUTUMN LEAF HUNT

—for the Eagle River Nature Center

Happy in the cold
gold day among the trees
holding hands

my daughter and I
hunt for a birch leaf
among the cottonwoods

that predominate,
that grow so big so fast
they overshadow

the deliberate pace
of the older paper birch:
Matter over mind?

The fallen leaves
all gold and heart-shaped,
are edge-distinguished—

the wavy cottonwood,
the birch pointed, like
arrayed arrows.

Forest-floor-kneeling,
my daughter asks, *If I'm
not Christian, then what?*

Atheist dad, agnostic mom,
brothers who favor
the Greek pantheon, she

adopted from a Buddhist country . . .
What sum minds, or matters,
in these trees?

CLOUDY DAY

This cold cloudy day comes to the Interior
like a case of beer from Tanana
or a scent of bear through the dog yard,
stimulating, a little dangerous maybe.

All day the sky holds its whiteness
overlapping the horizon like a stovepipe seam,
sealing, impressed, continuous, containing
smoke and creosote, building toward sudden
red. Sometime. Later. Maybe.

I think of the quintessential oriental landscape,
detail and mist and distance,
and signatures multiplying.

ALASKA VET'S CARIBOU DREAM

—for Tom

Me, up in the hills. Hunting caribou. Alone; no dogs.
> *Everything*
white, but warm.

Moved along pretty quick, crouched-like, with my
> *spotting-scope rifle.*
Once in a while, dropped down on one knee, used the scope
> *to scan the ridges.*

Spotted 'bou. Close. A whole bunch. Hunkered.
> *Point-blank range.*
Shot five or six. All went down. Pumped.

Started moving toward them. Spotted more
> *on a farther ridge.*
Fired. Two went down. Enough.

Made sense to cache the farthest kills first, come back
> *for the rest.*
Headed for the far hills. Everywhere, mist.

A field. No 'bou. Two peasants bleeding out
> *on the ground they'd been working*
with a small hand plow.

Turned back toward the first bunch: Saw velvet
on those antlers,
clear, through the scope.

Another field. Six dead peasants. No 'bou.
Started running.
Loping. Low. Quiet. Rifle light and loose.

Barrel balanced in my palm, moving a little,
like something alive.
Like a bird tied to my hand.

ECLIPSE OF AUTUMNAL MOTHS

—for Sijo

The morning after a full moon, we come,
my daughter and I, of a sudden, upon,
frozen into the now thinly iced pond,
what looks to be a cherry blossom path,
what looks to be a fairy blossom path,
tiny, papery, white petals strewn long.

It's past the time of blossoms. Past the time
of berries. And here above the tree line
near the top of Chugach State Park's
Baldy Mountain, we're beyond the reach
of destination-wedding flower baskets.
Mystified, entranced, we kneel, glad

for insulating pants, at the edge of the ice;
use the lenses on our iPhones to magnify
the unexplained phenomenon—see flight!
The petals are wings! These are moth bodies!
Flown into the reflected full-moon light
just as last night cooled and the pond iced.

Hundreds and hundreds, flat-pressed
between ice plates, like specimens
or keepsakes. Our fingers flutter like moth
wings on our camera shutters. Ping! Ping!
Ping! Ping! Ping! Ping! White feathery things
against dark water. Marvel. Metaphor.

NIGHT CONCERT

Dark woods invite with tricks of percussive might.
Boughs click-shift, lift, casting shadow-scores

across snowdrifts. Where boots crack thin ice
a snapping spreads. A syncopation threads. Nice.

Crunching snow. Gonging caws. A coyote yips. An owl
hoots. A human pants in breathy shiver-shudders.

Hooves drum. Spread wings strum. A scurry in dead
leaves adds an under-rhythm. And then there are

those sounds we can't quite hear but sense are there:
the thrum of hearts through bone and bark and stone.

WHEN BIRDS STOP SINGING

—for the Sally's Kitchen Singers

I

It's when the birds stop singing that people need to worry.
—Julian Treasure
My heart is like a singing bird.
—Christina Rossetti

We are bound,
on this found earth
by self-generated sound.

      I believe in singing.

Become one body
of resound, one instrument,
in intersectional vibration—

      We believe in singing.

grounding, bounding,
downing, astounding,
abounding in the round.

      Believe in singing.

Our mouths, our tongues,
our throats, our lungs,
made for sonic emanations.

      Hearts, singing birds.

Our ears, our minds,
our skin, our nerve endings,
made for sonic detecting.

Hearts, singing birds.

II

Nature is the one song of praise that never stops singing.
—Richard Rohr

Humans intone not alone.
Hear a caribou herd
panting en masse

Song of praise

across an Arctic plain—
for all the world a chanting
of cloaked Benedictines.

Song of praise

The soft and loud grunts and snorts,
the high calf bleats and bawls, the low
stag-hoots, bellows, rattles,

Song of praise

accompanied by winds,
percussive rain, rushing
glacial river cymbals . . .

Song of praise

and the humming, buzzing,
thrumming insects, the whistling,
calling, chirping, cawing birds,

Song of praise

the clitter-clatter chattering
scurryings of rodents,
the spouting of whales . . .

Song of praise

The symphonic chorus
all-around resounding,
porous, glorious, fulsome.

Song of praise

OPENINGS

—Shishmaref

We walk through the first
snow of the season, a fine
sifting—like meal—over every surface,
as to prevent dough sticking.

We walk through his village, a place
of clustered wooden structures; past
the old village site, where, now,
people in need dig for artifacts
to sell to outsiders for cash;
to the beach, a wind- and wave-swept
stretch of the Bering Strait, point
where east and west almost meet.

Glaucous gulls eye us with yellow eyes,
unraucously still. A lone raven sounds
two wooden flute notes. I complain.
Of doubts about my legitimacy. Fears.
Loneliness. Indirection. Of general
unhappiness. And he listens.

As he does, he picks tiny, spiraled shells
from the cold, snow-dusted sand, places
them into my cupped hands, one,
another, another one, and another,
places them open-side up so my eyes
fall into the curved spaces. Sand, snow
drop from shell-surface embossings
to catch in the warp of my wool mitts.

You *are* happy, he says, finally, to me,
when my words have all gone,
sifted down to join grain and crystal
on our particled wave of ground.
You only don't yet know it. You
are empty. To be so is to be open.
To whatever it is that follows.

III

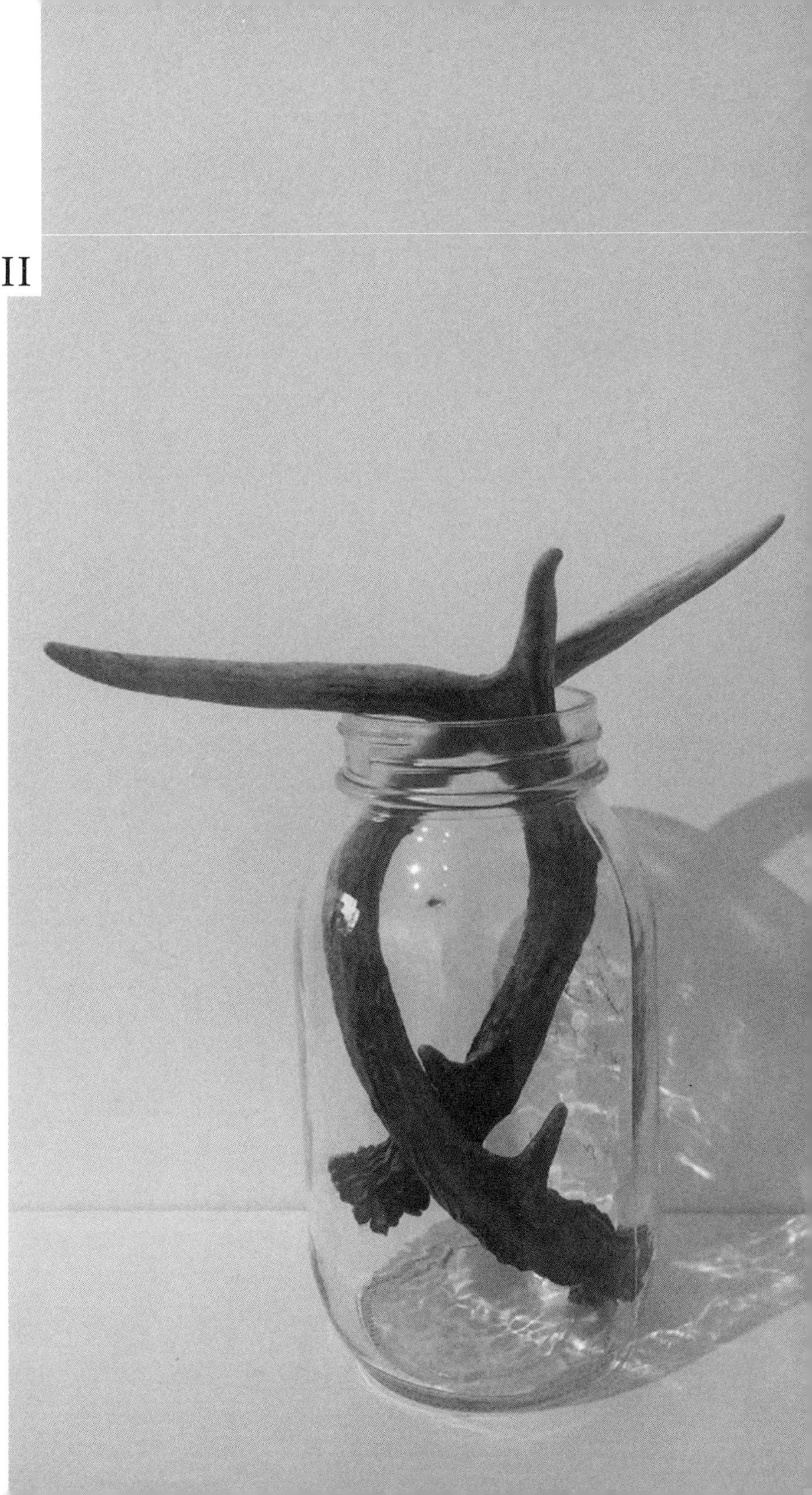

ABIDING
IN COLD

Cows no longer lactating, / bulls no longer sparring, / herd no longer moving, / south-of-the-tree-line snow / easily pawed from ground lichens . . . / Northern-forest-dispersed, / the herd thrives. Fattens.

NIGHT

Night in the north, lit
by a mirror of snow,
by featherings of ionized glow
swooping through the atmosphere-electric.

Night in the north crackles
through air and ice and smoke
searching between the angles
for wisps of individual angst.

Night arrives and the homeless receive it into their bones,
because it hones-in where they huddle in street alcoves:
Sometimes it needles, stings, a wasping
not possible to swat away, and potentially lethal.

Those who leave late know from frosted breath that
there will be no caress without consequence:
Booze, opiates, frictionless roads factor into
these nocturnal algorithms.

Night in the north, long,
carries a glittering blade
with which to cut out beating hearts
to animate—something else.

I BELIEVE

I believe it is for me
as a human being here
in this subarctic valley,
to greet black spruce,
hark tenacity, marvel
at gnarled darkness,
cradle cones in my hand, ahh
the way they ornament
the snow, offer themselves
to cold, their messages

always retold,
always differently,
always poems.

ORPHAN HOURS

Some nights, submerged leviathans,
intermittently recognized
by dorsal fin patterns,

break the surfaces of deep
marine dreams, breech,
occasioning rough wakes,

probing echolocations answered
by the hard-pounding notes
of the central organ.

~

Some nights, tined travelers
with ultraviolet-tuned eyes
recognize us dreamers

slumped under snowy sheets,
like lichens, waiting
to nourish something;

those deep blue winter eyes
see us in the dark
of our imaginings.

~

Some nights, death is just
the summer beach ice wave-stacked
between ocean, coastal plain.

Now, summer ice is not.
Eyes, memory, attest to change.
More than ice, going-going-gone.

When metaphors lose meaning
language, like any beast, becomes
endangered as a species.

~

And we are left to migrate
fluked or hooved through
dark dreams;

and we are left to our efforts
to dive or paw through
dense mediums;

and we are left to cry out
hoping to be, hoping
to be—answered.

AIYEE!

They are scarce this year, the moose
that in winters past have chewed our
willow, alder, have made in our clearing
snow nests, the moose that have lifted
the light of this valley into their antlers.

It is a time of scarce things, of scarce clean
earth, water, air, energy. There is now,
however, wherever, no scarcity
of consequences. And: *Whatever*
does not *whatsoever* cut it. *Please!*

A scarcity of the boundless-endless
joy of wild—of dried rosehip tea, of
preschool laminated-leaf placemats,
of being wildcam-paparazzi, of birch-sapping,
of berry-picking, of mushrooming—aiyee!

My gifted moccasins are old, but I remember
where they come from. The sky is not
uninvolved. Our scary masks, oh humans,
are slipping, slipping. Something
has rotted, wormed by greed.

The real people weep in their melting
houses without meeting the scarred,
the scared, minds of their sons, thinking
it is a strange way for the dance
that began with a drum bang, to end.

Between the scars of the people
and the scars of the earth
there is stretched sinew on which
time plays strange music—plays—
and everything, *everything,* sings.

SEAL HUNTERS

—Allakanuk

Ruffed men stand
on Bering ice, far
beyond the usual shore.
Under the day-moon,
drag their boats
(aluminum shimmers,
mirror-like signaling stars)
farther, farthest.

Winds did it,
blew ice hard against
the beaches, chunks like
mountains, frozen ridges
such that no
end can be seen. No seal
can claw, can push its breathing
through this.

They stop. And kneel.
Chip with spears until
they break through. Jig for cod.
Bring back, each, seventy
or eighty,
pounds of finned and scaled flesh.
Darkly mounded, the boats
dragged home are eyes.

ASTRONOMY LESSON

The group stands in couples, like palms, sea breezes lifting
whatever lies loose upon us. The Maui-Hyatt astronomer
remarks upon the Alaska-made telescope secured rooftop
nine floors up; its state-of-the-art mechanics. We glow
our pride of home-place, my husband and I, as we breathe in,
here, that warm-dark that is, there, oxymoronic. As we lean in:
University-quality, the cosmologist beams, *computerized,*
with a unique focus, binocular-like, user-friendly, clearest
sky images you will ever have seen. We smile at how earnest.
I'm entering the computer code for the moon, he says.
This telescope magnifies ninety times. You will see each
bump and crater. The moon's reflected light will be blinding
as headlights. We bound and jostle to be deer. Magnified
ninety times, I think. A good-genes lifetime. Might insight
be just this: enlarging, year by year, the inner mirror?

EVENING STEAM

—Togiak

There come to me the voices
of Yupik women in the steamy dark
where they bead their skins
with a water born of fire,
beads that pull into threads
stitching over skins like lace
veils that net and knot,
place and pull from place.

Outside, children's voices
drop into the night like ice
shattering onto the road
from house eaves.
Someone names each child.
On my lips my tongue tastes salt.
Words lose to laughter:
sharpness to dissolve.

A basin is passed, a cloth, a dipper,
a bucket of cool water.
From the melding of molecules,
we reclaim our momentary skins.

CABIN QUEEN

—for Buddha

With a wooden scepter made in Indonesia,
in oil pressed from olives grown in Spain,
she stirs chunks of caribou harvested by her husband,
into leeks farmed by friends. And garlic.

The boreal incense wafts toward the ones who drink beer
and play computer games and music.
Others are expected to appear at the door soon   starving
as young ones always are.   Growing.

It is necessary then to shed skins to step thin
through boots scattered by the others already in
to the same warmth and light that draws the flies that hide
in the drying cracks of the house logs.

The micro-aviators survive deepened cold
seeking and finding seeming safe haven and then
fry themselves against alluring tubed-fluorescents.
Collect upon diffuser panels.   Chaffed.

At the queen's unignorable request
tall sons reach up with long arms   to angle
the frosted panels, to let crisped insects drop
into a waiting dustpan.   Gone,

after inspection of their dried-leaf carcasses,
into the soil rooting the leafing that encircles
the closed-eyed Buddha, who calms the queen,
reminding her to breathe: In. Out. In.

TOWARD PLEIADES

Against the tow line
harnesses clink.
Furred feet pound on snow.
The sound of panting.

A hum. A whistle.
Driver leaning
easy in the sway.
Who is leading?

In the basket: me,
shimmying over
packed trail, toward Pleiades.
And who is caught?

MAN, WOMAN, CORVUS

—for Eric

When we make our long scratches in the snow,

like birds dragging their feet,

we signal, to something with a point of perspective,

our narrow-track persistence.

To the circling, perching ravens, if not other or else,

they of feathers that rustle

like silk, of complex vocabularies echoing in the hills.

And how far do our own

sounds carry? Our argument: Should this man, tall,

ski ahead to break trail,

or she, the shorter, so both can enjoy the 'scape?

Today in the paper NASA announced

a Goldilocks-zone planet.

Some six hundred light years away, it would take a shuttle

22 million years

to reach. Require a categorical explosion

of intergalactic

space travel, auto-navigation, cryogenics,

to ever dream of splashing

in its 72-degree oceans rippling in every direction.

For sure we can't ski there.

Ravens won't be winging it I'd guess.

Now the tall man whistles to the corvids,

trading imitation

for imitation. The woman swings ahead, says:
My love for you has grown
into the landscape, and multiplied. Like syllables,
fresh flakes pass through space,
clump into energized tropes that stun, melt
wetly on exposed faces,
accumulate, on common ground. An agreement
can sometimes be found
where inter- and intra-species share tracks.

PRESSED TO THE EARTH

Under sled runners, a dead cone,

wrested,

scatters seeds across hardpack,

grinning fangs sinking

darkly, warmly, into snow. Sweet

sharp bite, slow,

leaving no mark but

ready to explode

in time.

        In time we

are all cones

sending bullets into flesh,

all seeds,

wrested and wresting

      to bite

      to burst.

LITTLE CHURCH ON THE RIVER

Snow falls still,
masses notwithstanding.

Sills all fill,
ledge-width notwithstanding.

Windows gape dark,
stained glass notwithstanding.

Willows lace stark,
white trace notwithstanding.

    Little girls faint
    watching flames can-can
    into haloed space.

    Little girls faint
    watching wax ribbons
    unfurl slowly scarring
    virgin marypoles.

    Little girls faint
    watching flames flinch
    at flapping silken vestments
    slapping air from
    holy heels.

Little girls faint
watching altar boys work
wafers stuck on rooftops:
Careful, if you chew
you're a God-killer.

Little girls think
God I'm so crazy
for him I can't wait
to go to bed, so I can
dream . . .

Winter, windows freeze shut
like the river. Wood
dries brittle. Winter ends,
but in slivers.

SNOW MACHINE COLLISION
—*February 11, 2015*

snow   falling falling falling
on the   thirty-mile winter trail
between Ambler   and Shungnak

two   Inupiat   villages
of less than three hundred   residents
each   nets   of relations

knotted to the river the Kobuk
which offers a million pounds of
twenty-three   fish species

~

two   Ambler   girl-cousins
set off   on a snow machine revving
into the   seasonal   dark

to play   basketball
to raise money   for funeral costs
for two   Shungnak elders

I say: girls. I have   such a girl-
woman-early-twenties daughter:
Hi Mommy!   *Bye Mommy*

~

Hi Auntie!   *Bye Auntie!*
and away the cousins go   into the dark
until   midway   a head-to-head

the passenger   flies over
her cousin   over the old man   he
who mumbles   smells   of liquor

no peace   in the memory
of   sweetness   bleeding into the night
from   ears   nose   mouth

~

the cousin thrown   scrambles
to the bleeding-seizing-retching   sister
pats her   with shaking hands

for a cellphone   palms it   weeping
runs for higher ground   seeking
                    cell reception and

sees   approaching   lights turns back
flags   those passing   screaming
Help!   *Help!*   *Help!*

~

those passing   radio on their VHF
and the cousin standing   wraps the cousin
splayed   with all she has

shields her   as best she can
from the heat-thieving wind   bends
over the girl's head   deadweight   in her lap

waits waits waits   for help
murmuring   *I'm here with you*   *hold on*
hold on   hold on   cousin . . .

~

the unconscious girl   is loaded
onto a snow-machine-drawn sled
rushed   to her village clinic

her auntie   squeezes a ventilation bag
while EMTs   spread the girl's ribs
put   a tube   into her chest

keeping her alive   keeping her
alive   the hours it takes   for the medevac
plane   to arrive

~

from the air   it is clear
how the trail   parallels the river
from the air   on a clear day

going out   unconscious
coming back   in a body bag   she
didn't get to see it that way

never   opened her eyes
after   that impact surprise
that   locking   of snow machine skis

~

the village remembers her good
    going out and getting wood
    going out and   picking berries

    cleaning up for people
cooking   meals for students
    in the school cafeteria

loving her family   her mother her auntie
loving   her longtime boyfriend
loving   her two children

~

her   handsome young lover
of an age with my boy-man sons   father
of her children   4 and 5

steeps   his sorrow   his fury
in drink   his despair   his sadness
becomes   everything   and

two months after   he shoots himself
leaving the grandparents to raise
orphaned   siblings

~

leaving the cousin to   each day
pass the old man   his machine
while law enforcement does   nothing

leaving us to think how   all the world's
light   and all the world's dark
can fit into an eye   into a heart

leaving us to think about the snow   about
the sky   on the thirty-mile winter trail
       between Ambler and Shungnak

LANDSCAPE WITH PISSING DUDE

—after Lorca's poem about New York City,
"Landscape of a Pissing Multitude"

The woman keeps on,

slowly ascending the mountain,

not waiting for the man who lags behind.

The woman keeps on,

breaking trail through new snow,

expecting to be caught up by the longer strider.

The woman keeps on,

dreaming of branches turning into antlers,

of moths frozen into the light of reflected moons.

The woman keeps on,

her steps punching craters through crust,

her breaths crystalizing into clouds.

The woman keeps on,

chasing the purity of the scene she's entered;

embracing the calm witness of all things.

The woman keeps on,

because, against it, that cold sky-blue,

obscurity is insured.

The woman keeps on,

switching back as elevation demands,

the cure for lungs so expanded.

The woman keeps on

toward that peak that pierces its heart

to effect a calling cairn.

The woman keeps on,

to turn, breathless, at the line of the ridge,

ambushed by landscape and silence.

The man, stopped below,

spreads his legs, lowers his head, aims his

hisssssssss, into—what?

POEM HOME

—for my father, a counterpoint to
Jim Heynan's "Iowa Poem"

Winter, and Dad writes
from neighborhood Chicago,
How's the weather up there?
Have you found a good-paying job?

What can I say?
The weather, Dad, it's cold.
The angle of light, always low,
melts only a little of the rim
between sky-white and snow.
Things come together here, Dad,
more and less than anyplace else.
Moose pay me well—yes—
to follow in their tracks.
I split wood and poems
spring from my hand,
each warming in its own way.

Your work is your life.
Can you, will you, understand
my life as my work?

Dad, let me say, *Don't worry.*
I'll be all right, *here or there.*
In my heart there lives still
the immigrant determined
to make good. What better goal
than warmth in cold, warmth—
of food, of wood, of word?

ROADKILL

Snow did it.
Dumped on mountains.
Brought moose down
to cleared roads,
to browse over guardrails
on weed willow.

A curve
          limited sight.
A hill
          frustrated braking.

Four at one spot
in one day.
Decapitated on-site:
heads to DFG;
bodies to charities,
crushed bones extracted
from macerated meat
for soup.

What's left,
ravens collect.

RIVER SKI SONG

Let me begin
by singing how
I skied the river,
today, as the sun slipped
back of the near ridge. I
stretched my steps like snares
in trails made by snow machines,
trails leading everywhere
in gamey loops. I made
more, in the air, in
my swallow-heart
knowing: what
sets, rises.

Rises, or
sets something rising.
I saw color clumped in aspen
on the islands, on the facing hills.
Willows held it on northeastern shores.
My face caught it, moving toward
the disappearing source. In pinkness
I stopped, landing lightly,
dropping wings against my
down-protected body.
And I held it:

The odd

  feeling rising in me,

  standing still in the darkening,

  that the sun had set in me; standing

  there, on snow over ice, I felt myself

  glowing; felt the living leaning, leaning

  toward me; recalled, believing,

  the ancient Greek theory that

  humans throw light, our eyes

  small suns, always gleaming.

  I am telling you now,

  how I skied home.

RIFFLES

The dredge sits frozen in its own water,
stilled by the gold prices
before the ice.

Iron buckets hang, an endless chain—
eyeless sockets,
vacant.

Once they scooped rocks and earth like
water, poured
rocks and earth

like water, over sluice slides, shooting
swaths of water over
rocks and earth.

Riffles trapped gold like fat thoughts,
the rest floating
to a belt

that threw high and to the sides
with sweeping
sure swings;

changing this landscape for a ride,
that dizzied
and dropped.

TWO WAYS WITH SNOW

(i.)

In the valley snow sifts like meal,
drifts over tussocks, trails, scrawny spruce,

dusts shapes as with time or distance, makes
place a dream—lovely, sad, fading.

Lakes fill like rice bowls. Rivers, sloughs, creeks
lie well-spread with caulk. Every, all, caressed—softly

  effaced.

(ii.)

On the flats wind hardpacks, punches meal
into thick-crusted bread. High loaves, glazed

as with butter. I am raised above the trees
to meet the fist, to meet the pounding

of cloud-grist, with impartial earnest, with zeal,
into smoothness, beauty, pain—

  reshaped.

UNDER THE SCOPE

—Fort Yukon

Slick streets shine

like mirrors,

evenly lighting

earthly specimens.

On the slide,

I jig.

FACING THE STARS

—for David Ignatow

I face the stars
in an empty tundra flat, no one
for miles near, no one knowing
I am here

so that I do not exist other
than in memory and expectation;

except to the dogs that pull me,
the snow, the tussocks
that bear our weight, air
sucked and blown in our breathing,
ravens flying over,
lemmings burrowing under,
the wolf, fox, lynx, marten—
that wonder
what I am up to
with my bundled sled;

and except for my own mind
that is not frightened of itself
in the silent space, facing the stars
that to themselves are
so woefully adequate.

CHASING THE LIGHTS

Here, area hotels offer
northern lights wake-up calls.

But, more even than the tourists,
we who live here long to see
the streaming sun particles
strike our magnetic field,
charge across dark. Surge,
pulse, whip, writhe. Relax.

Cocooned in home-stitched quilts,
we drive north in chase, listening
to streaming notes made
by fingers striking keys,
tones furling, spiraling
—aching to resolve.

HOUSE FLIES WATCH HER BRING IN THE PAPER

Before going out she slips her feet into zippered boots,
sits to pull on ice-grippers,
selects a coat to match the weather,
which is most often gelid.

We watch her from the window, loping over rutted snow,
a well-padded arm-swinging beast
lumbering up the drive between
snow-belled elderberry,

crowding against the split rail fence, lit equinox to equinox
with looped strings of little white lights,
on the other side, cottonwoods,
young alders bent to form dens.

We watch, thinking to ourselves: Why is she making this
little lap in the cold and dark
when there is warmth within,
where we await her return?

IF WE COULD

The moon each month grows new antlers,
drops velvet into the night and,
under foot-thick river ice, sleek beaver fur
parts the dark to carve stars of birch limbs,
of alder, spruce, and willow shoots, and to
eat the shining, and perhaps to be snared
into the light, for blankets and dog food.
We would snare the moon, too, if we could.
You know we would. You know. We would.

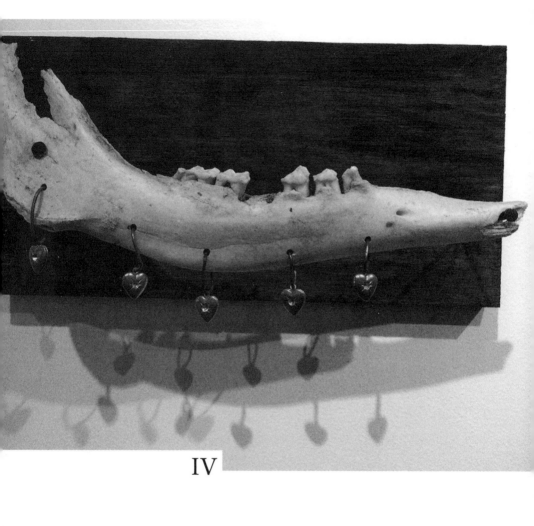

IV

NORTH TOWARD COOLING
CALVING GROUNDS

Late-winter snowmelt triggers the migration / of antsy pregnant cows anxious to reach / the soothing succor of the sea-ice breezes / that sweep, constantly, the relatively / predator-free, food-rich Arctic coastal plain, / the breezes that inhibit the otherwise unrelieved / torment of spring-summer insects; / the migration of cows heavy with their stirrings, / straining for the frosty Paradise into which calves / must be born to survive, the timing so crucial: / imperative to beat spring break-up north, / its taxing and dangerous open-river / crossings, its mud-miring, its permafrost sinks. / Bulls, yearlings, dry cows meander after, they / the less vulnerable, the less herd-future critical, / the moving meat, the ethical take for humans. / The caribou, they stir to remain in the sweet soul-mate / embrace of the cold; retreat from meltings, from / softenings, from earth phases / in which they cannot flourish. /

BEHOOVED MOTHERS

—for Gideon James who shared the Gwich'in
word, for the Gwich'in Steering Committee, and
for "the Mothers"

Kiekailic—the tight team

of mature cows who take turns

leading the caribou herd

from winter woods

to spring calving plains.

> *kiekailic, kiekailic*

The vanguard always

allowed to pass through,

because how would the rest

know how to come back, how

to find the migration path?

> *kiekailic, kiekailic*

The traditional knowledge

that the leading group navigates,

that the rest just stick together,

using herd cues—rediscovered,

now, by Western science.

> *kiekailic, kiekailic*

The Gwich'in word, it mimics

the clicking slip of 'bou tendons

over sesamoid foot bones,

a sound akin to the wit

of quick finger snapping. Bit

kiekailic, kiekailic

of a curious adaptation,

keeping caribou in constant

audio contact, through all impediments

of visibility—snow, sleet,

rain, fog, insect clouds . . .

kiekailic, kiekailic

A son writes a symphony

in which one instrumental

voice takes over from another

to honor the rotating leaders,

we behooved old mothers:

kiekailic.

SPRING SKI SONG

—for Erin

Where the trail opens

    onto flats, into

        sun-softened snow,

through the flutterings

    of suddenly living

        dusty-winged moths,

I slide on waxed wood

    into—light,

        into—hot.

Miles lie flat and white

    and far, on all sides,

        to the mountains, and

knowing no soul lives

    anywhere near or

        could possibly appear

without warning I
        pull off my shirt and
                put up my hair and

swing along feeling
        sweet-sighted by light,
                sweet-tasted by warm,

sweet-touched by air.
        My poles make two rows
                of dimples. A moth wing

brushes my nipple, causing
        me to sing. I keep
                going and going.

INTERIOR

—for my two home-places, Alaska and Lietuva

I fly in, this first Arctic spring, like a bird
migrating a yearning rather than a route, landing
among multiple small mirrors, flashing-flashing
seizures of epigenetic memory.

All that angled light haloing the soft hills,
the new leafing of birch and spruce, the complex
scent of stovepipe smoke, rising-rising
from that forgotten place where hearths blazed.

And the river, its fair banks defining,
connecting, place and time, places and times.
Me, here, now, I get the little-hairs-rising feeling
about a life I haven't lived, but might.

Above, long-necked, long-legged avians fly in Vs,
a shape both convex and concave. I weep
as my grandmother wept, her tears seeping
from the corners of my eyes, over the soft sides

of a face that recognizes: These are not storks,
but cranes. Both be harbingers of fortune.
That day becomes a golden egg, with its seed
of a winged mind, its sequence of northern—

according to 23 and Me—European
DNA, snaking like a river through
the ages, keeping me indigenous
to that other-occupied land I'd never seen.

LIKE MOUNTAIN SNOWMELT

—for Katy, Sharman, Paula, Sarah, Diane

We let down our milk
as we let down our hair,
with the same little breath,
the soft settling
of the muscles, faces calming
like pools after wind.

Our milk releases
like mountain snowmelt
suckled by sun,
as rivers unbraid
toward melding.

IN MY DREAMS

—for the Bear Mountain folk

When ursine heft lumbers
across our cedar deck, every board
laid by my husband's hand; when
bruin eyes press myopically
against the expanse of glass we
angled to catch the southern light;
when whoofs startle the small son
blowing bubbles over grass
with a star wand—I take fright.

Yet, in my dreams I wear that bear
skin. I break things, rake flesh,
am weighty and lithe, and others
run or stand still, but do not try
to play with me. When I wake,
I recall that the same river draws
us each with its hidden rushings.
I imagine matching smudge for
smudge on opposite sides

of the great-room window. Eye-
to-eye what would we see? I hear
women have married bears.
How many, with berry-stained
lips, wish to wear their furred
hides? What woman doesn't
wish she could sleep away winter
to wake hungry again in spring?
Oh spring! Oh spring! Oh spring!

THREE RULES

The river changes course each spring, is
called crazy, *tozitna*, just for this defiance of knowing.
Freed by sun, fed by snow, its force
flows through thinning ice, cracks mass into floes,
tosses ton-chunks to shore like confining notions,
scraping off banks of willows as if shadows,
making new islands, fresh sloughs.

In a quiet, wood-warmed house, visiting over
pilot bread, fish strips, coffee, a Tanana woman
passes me, like cards, three rules to play
against the crazy future:
        Don't talk.
        Be ready.
        Laugh.
Oil of fish glowing on her lips,
she says exactly this:
        Don't talk about the future;
        aiyee, you'll jinx it.
        When it comes, it comes.
        You keep your eyes open.
        If it is easy, you laugh,
        and be easy.
        If it is hard, you laugh,
        and be hard.

THE DAY THE TRIPOD FELL

Windshields radiant with rain
reflect budding birch. Prayer
flags pretend to be returned
songbirds intent on flapping
games. Hair offers nesting fibers.
Steps spring of themselves
into miraculous mud, with such
a luscious suck and smack
that even rigid river ice can't
help but—what?   up.
                 Crack

ABOUT NAMING

—for Karen

We slush to the new-melted slough
accompanied by child and dog
to name the birds.
We take cheese and apples and words
past-crafted to conjure:
Pintail, shoveler, goldeneye.
Our fingers point like wands, our tongues
shape incantations: Blessings.
On the birds, the men, the women who
first named, on the time, the space
                    between.

We draw meaning like breath,
passing it throat to throat and back.

We eat our apples, cheese, suck handfuls
of clean snow from shadows, allow
ripples of feathered landings to fade
onto irises, fluttering light
into wakeful patterns.

THE FIELD

—a response to Jane Draycott's poem "The Square"

Across the field, a cow moose peers at me
from a door framed by trees. The gloom
of the forest room sweeps her forward.

In her fitted, furred hide, *she is beautiful,*
glassy black heels parting the grass,
like my grandmother, *before I knew her.*

Between us a treacherous sea, waves lifting
fear and need toward a beckoning statue,
a shape only faintly, only barely, discerned.

Like a statue, or a tree, across the field, *I*
return her look impassively, my sass
arrested by her imprinted caution.

When I cross that liminal sea to her forest
what will I find in the staked shadows?
Will I reach my row of new willows?

PINGO POEM

On the ridge,
I point at pingos; blue
eyes glint, tell me

Rocks there are so
old you have to kiss
them. Yes.

I look away,
lean against birch.
Less than hum.

On a duck's back
I fly toward summer,
or midnight

in a green marsh,
tremble-bright,
holding hands.

I wrinkle my nose,
flare it. You crinkle
your eyes, bare

them. A secret
recipe we share
for rainbows

with spring
greens. I try
to persuade you

to eat with your
fingers. You prefer
mine.

~

I think of my
friend, a
surgeon's son,

hit by a car while
driving his grandmother
to town.

She dies. He:
coma. A lawyer.
Should I whisper

in his ear: limitation
is the mother
of greatness?

The employer?
Heartbeat or hum?
A rainbow in a pan?

A Dalmatian leaps
in snow: A flight of perfectly
synchronized birds.

A seeping
into tiny cracks
creates ice wedges.

~

My finches died
on their backs, claws
curled like fists.

In the Juneau museum
Indian dolls with
bird claw fingers

remind me
of Grandma K who
pinched my arms and thighs.

She had her joke:
She wouldn't eat me
unless I fattened.

A golden mean
to wield against flesh-eaters
and oven death.

~

Off the ridge
pingos point at me.
I hide in books.

I look for false
dilemmas, and I
find them.

Today the story
of a gym instructor
skating with his class.

He fell through thin ice.
Students gathered round
for the lesson:

Stay in the water,
freeze; crawl out—freeze.
Unless . . .

Ideas spread across
closed lids. Still-damp
hair, fanned softly

bright across
the pillow. Lines like nets.
Traditions.

There is an Inside
Passage. Eagles found
it—I

saw the white spots
in dark spruce. Who
told the old woman

they are plastic
bleach bottles hung
to fool tourists?

Dilemmas
push out poems
like pingos.

When they are
high enough, I
climb them

for exercise.
We can climb
together

if you don't mind
moving slowly.
Watch

the sandhill cranes
fold, unfold,
their great wings.

~

I saw his limbs
swell. Nerves pounded codes
against a closed brain. I

cried, like a hawk.
Does the flying duck
wish it could stay?

You ride your bicycle
on ice. You fall.
I slide.

I read of blonde girls
straight As and in love
with vampires.

A friend thinks they
could be weaned
to artificial blood.

Like hunting bear with
airplanes, I say. Leads
to alcoholism.

How do water, earth, and air
fill space
with grace?

You and me
heartbeats and hums,
maybe

someday a song.
It is spring, yet I have
snow in mind.

AN AFTERWORD

OH!

Oh, that blue pearl!
The world   at home in the busy sky—
we hold it   to our throats.

That lustrous seed,
turning   in an ocean of milky rivers
teeming   with tined fruits.

That curved hoof
that wrestles   life from mire,
that murmur   of a mouth.

ACKNOWLEDGMENTS

The noted poems appeared first in the following publications: *Permafrost* and the anthology *Top of the World/poetryALASKAwomen* ("Roads") [The poem "Roads" was also twice set to music, first by composer Cynthia Folio as part of the song cycle "At the Edge of Great Quiet" for chorus and piano and then by composer Andrea Clearwater as part of the song cycle "The Drift of Things; Winter Songs" scored for baritone and piano]; *Cirque* ("A Shadow," "Women Boating," "Three Rules"); *Southwest Anthology* (an earlier version of "Implicated"); *Cotton Boll/ Atlantic Review* ("Utqiaġvik Beach Walk" under the title "Barrow Beach Walk"); *Fairbanks Daily News-Miner* and the "Ten Poets" 2018 broadside show (an earlier version of "What Is Wild"); calendar ("Addressing the Glacier"); *Alaska Women Speak* (an earlier version of "Vision Dream"); *Saturday Night* ("About Skies"); International Gallery of Contemporary Art Show (an earlier version of "Eclipse of Autumnal Moths"); *Cabin* ("Evening Steam"); *Northward Journal* ("Two Ways With Snow," "Raven"); *49 Writers/Alaska Shorts* ("Facing the Stars," "River Ski Song," "Addressing the Glacier"); *Poetaster* ("Facing the Stars"); anthology: *Flights of Fancy* ("About Naming"). All of the above poems were published under the name Mary Kancewick.

The cover features a work from Sonya Kelliher-Combs's *Remnant* series: *Remnant (Caribou Antler)*, 2016, used with the permission of the artist. All interior photographs were taken by the author and used with the permission of the artists/ museums. "Context Is Everything" (taken in 2018) features a caribou skull mounted on a barn wall at the Alaska Wildlife Conservation Center. Part I opener features a stacked caribou rack work by Wanda Chin (2005), part of the permanent exhibit at the University of Alaska Museum of the North. Part II features dance fans made by Katie Tootlook (of Bethel) from coiled tapernaq grass, green yarn, caribou beard, and goose feathers; photographed at the Yupiit Piciryarait Museum in Bethel, Alaska, and part of the Swanson collection donated in the 1970s. Part III, featuring antlers in a canning jar, is a work from Hollis Mickey's *Root Cellar* show; photographed during an exhibition at the International Gallery of Contemporary Art (IGCA) in 2017. Part IV features a work from Katherine Coons's *Raw Natures* series; photographed during an exhibition at the IGCA in 2017. "An Afterword" features a Hollis Mickey embroidery piece entitled "The skin of winter fruits," exhibited at the IGCA in 2017. The title of this work was inspired by Sheila Wyne's *Adaptation* series, exhibited at the Alaska Humanities Forum in 2014.

I want to thank Nate, Krista, and Laura of University of Alaska Press, and press proofreader Joeth, for doing their manuscript-to-book magic; and to thank Peggy Shumaker and the Alaska Literary Series readers and board for their confidence in my work. A thank-you also to the members of the Ten Poets group, for their careful reading of and response to a number of these poems, and to Jeremy Pataky, Executive Director of 49 Writers, for his wise counsel on this journey. Special thank-yous to my husband, Eric, for his sustaining love and support; to my son Matthew, the first reader of the first version of this book, who helped me to see the whole as greater than the sum of its parts; to my son David, who made of the poem "Roads" a song we could all sing; to my daughter, Sijo, a fellow poet, who inspired a number of these poems; and to Melissa Nix, for her generous early proofreading.

MAR KA lives and writes from the foothills of Alaska's Chugach Mountains. As an indigenous rights attorney, she has traveled to villages throughout this largely wilderness state. She is the recipient of an NEH grant and the Midnight Sun Poetry Prize. Her poems have been published in national and international journals and anthologies, and on occasion set to music. She is a graduate of Northwestern University's Medill School of Journalism (BSJ), University of Chicago Law School (JD), and the Institute of American Indian Arts (MFA). Mar Ka is of Lithuanian heritage. This is her first book.